Fathers Change the World . . . One Child at a Time

Fathers Change the World . . . One Child at a Time

A Treasury of Fatherly Wisdom

by Dr. Criswell Freeman

DELANEY STREET PRESS
Nashville, TN: (800) 256-8584

ISBN 1-58334-057-2

The ideas expressed in this book are not, in all cases, exact quotations, as some have been edited for clarity and brevity. In all cases, the author has attempted to maintain the speaker's original intent. In some cases, material for this book was obtained from secondary sources, primarily print media. While every effort was made to ensure the accuracy of these sources, the accuracy cannot be guaranteed. For additions, deletions, corrections or clarifications in future editions of this text, please write DELANEY STREET PRESS.

Cover Design by Bart Dawson
Layout by Swan Lake Communications,
Jackson, Mississippi

Printed in the United States of America

1 2 3 4 5 6 7 8 9 10 • 00 01 02 03 04 05 06

ACKNOWLEDGMENTS

The author gratefully acknowledges the helpful support of Angela Beasley Freeman, Dick and Mary Freeman, Mary Susan Freeman, Jim Gallery, and the entire team of professionals at DELANEY STREET PRESS and WALNUT GROVE PRESS.

For Dick Freeman,
Harvey Freeman,
and Bill Criswell

Table of Contents

Introduction

Fathers influence the world by influencing their children. Using quotations from a wide assortment of notable men, this little book chronicles nine timeless lessons that any father would be proud to teach.

Life is sometimes difficult for all of us. The fatherly advice on these pages is intended to provide insight and inspiration for the hard times as well as the good times.

So whether you're a father, grandfather, great-grandfather, or grateful child, take these words of wisdom to heart.

And as you read these pages, perhaps you'll understand once and for all how fathers change the world — one child at a time.

Love

The first gift a caring father gives his child is the gift of love. This gift begins before birth, extends throughout life, and endures long after death.

Lessons of love are taught not by word but by deed, and a father's love, freely given, is a lasting legacy to the world.

The following quotations clearly demonstrate that love, especially the love of a father for his family, can last a lifetime — and beyond.

Love is ever
the beginning of
knowledge as fire
is of light.

THOMAS CARLYLE

Life is the flower of which love is the honey.

VICTOR HUGO

Love is Nature's second sun.

GEORGE CHAPMAN

If a thing loves, it is infinite.

WILLIAM BLAKE

Love is the essence of God.

RALPH WALDO EMERSON

He who is filled with love is
filled with God Himself.
ST. AUGUSTINE

Love is the river of life in this world.
HENRY WARD BEECHER

Love

Discover someone to help
    shoulder your misfortunes.
Then, you will never be alone.
Neither fate, nor the crowd,
    so readily attacks two.

BALTASAR GRACIÁN

We are all born for love;
    it is the principle of existence
        and its only end.

BENJAMIN DISRAELI

Love, and you shall be loved.
    All love is mathematical,
just as much as the two sides
    of an algebraic equation.

RALPH WALDO EMERSON

Bitterness imprisons life; love releases it.

HARRY EMERSON FOSDICK

Love is the
ultimate and
the highest goal
to which man
can aspire.

VICTOR FRANKL

All mankind loves a lover.

RALPH WALDO EMERSON

Life's greatest happiness
is to be convinced we are loved.

VICTOR HUGO

For those passionately in love,
the whole world seems to smile.

DAVID MYERS

The one thing we can never get
enough of is love. And the one thing
we can never give enough of is love.

HENRY MILLER

Love is the only sane and
satisfactory answer to the problems
of human existence.

ERICH FROMM

Love may not last forever
but it lingers.

ROBERT FULGHUM

Love is the subtlest force in the world.

MOHANDAS GANDHI

One cannot give what he does not
possess. To give love you must
possess love. To love others
you must love yourself.

LEO BUSCAGLIA

If you can't stand yourself,
neither can anybody else.

SID CAESAR

To be loved, love.

DECIMUS MAXIMUS AUSONIUS

Let my heart be wise.
It is the gods' best gift.

EURIPIDES

Love gives itself;
it is not bought.

LONGFELLOW

Love is primarily giving,
not receiving.

ERICH FROMM

Love is an active verb –
　　a river, not a pond.
　　　　　ROBERT FULGHUM

Love is an activity, not a passive
　　affect; it is a "standing in,"
　　　not a "falling for."
　　　　　ERICH FROMM

Love seeks one thing only:
　　the good of the one loved.
It leaves all the other secondary
effects to take care of themselves.
Love, therefore, is its own reward.
　　　　　THOMAS MERTON

We are shaped and fashioned
by what we love.

GOETHE

A man is only as good
as what he loves.

SAUL BELLOW

Passion is a bad counselor.

THOMAS HARDY

One can only obey the great law
of the heart that says, "As long as
you live, love one another and
take the consequences."

ROBERT FULGHUM

Love does not dominate;
it cultivates.

GOETHE

Life is a romantic business,
but you have to make the romance.

OLIVER WENDELL HOLMES, SR.

Hatred darkens life;
      love illuminates it.
          MARTIN LUTHER KING, JR.

By the accident of fortune,
a man may rule the world for a time,
   but by virtue of love he may rule
       the world forever.
             LAO-TZU

Neither a lofty degree of
  intelligence nor imagination nor
both together go to the making of
genius. Love, love, love, that is
    the soul of genius.
    WOLFGANG AMADEUS MOZART

Love is the crowning grace of
humanity, the holiest
right of the soul.

PETRARCH

Real love is a permanently
self-enlarging experience.

M. SCOTT PECK

Nothing we do, however virtuous,
can be accomplished alone;
therefore we are saved by love.

REINHOLD NIEBUHR

Love is the fire of life;
 it either consumes or purifies.

ANONYMOUS

Love is as strong as death.

SONG OF SOLOMON 8:6

Love is the only gold.

ALFRED, LORD TENNYSON

The best portion of a good man's
life is his little, nameless,
unremembered acts of kindness
and of love.

WILLIAM WORDSWORTH

Who, being loved, is poor?

OSCAR WILDE

And now abideth faith, hope, love,
these three; but the
greatest of these is love.

I CORINTHIANS 13:13

FATHER'S LESSON #2

Family

A father serves many roles. He is a leader, teacher, disciplinarian, bread-winner, motivator, entertainment director, voice of reason, and, above all, standard-bearer for the family.

On the pages that follow, we examine one of the most important lessons that any father can teach: what it means to be a family.

A happy family
is but an earlier heaven.

SIR JOHN BOWRING

Other things may change us,
but we start and end
with the family.

ANTHONY BRANDT

A family is a school of duties...
founded on love.

FELIX ADLER

The family is the nucleus of civilization.

WILL AND ARIEL DURANT

Blessed indeed is the man who
hears many gentle voices
call him father!

LYDIA MARIA CHILD

A family is a court of justice
which never shuts down,
for night or day.

MALCOLM DE CHAZAL

Family life is the source of the
greatest human happiness.

ROBERT J. GAVINGHURST

It takes a heap
of livin' in a house
to make it
home.

EDGAR A. GUEST

Home, in one form or another,
is the great objective of life.

JOSIAH G. HOLLAND

The happiest moments of my life
have been spent in the bosom
of my family.

THOMAS JEFFERSON

When the whole family
is together, the soul is in place.

RUSSIAN PROVERB

B etter a hundred enemies outside
the house than
one inside.

ARABIAN PROVERB

A good laugh is sunshine
in the house.

WILLIAM MAKEPEACE THACKERAY

A ll happy families resemble
one another; every unhappy family
is unhappy in its own way.

LEO TOLSTOY

A family is one of nature's masterpieces.

GEORGE SANTAYANA

You don't
choose your family.
They are God's gift
to you, as you
are to them.

DESMOND TUTU

When brothers agree, no fortress
is so strong as their common life.
ANTISTHENES

Children are the hands
by which we take hold of heaven.
HENRY WARD BEECHER

A child is a beam of sunlight from
the Infinite and Eternal.
LYMAN ABBOTT

What we desire our children
to become, we must endeavor
to be before them.

ANDREW COMBE

Raising children is not unlike
a long-distance race in which the
contestants must learn to pace
themselves. That is the
secret of winning.

JAMES C. DOBSON

Lucky that man whose children
make his happiness in life.

EURIPIDES

The best things
you can give
children next to
good habits are
good memories.

SYDNEY J. HARRIS

Upon our children — how
they are taught — rests the fate,
or fortune, of tomorrow's world.

B. C. FORBES

The most important thing
a father can do for his children is
to love their mother.

REV. THEODORE M. HESBURGH

Children have more need of
models than critics.

JOSEPH JOUBERT

Examine yourselves — ask,
each of you, "Have I been a good
brother? . . . son? . . . husband? . . .
father? . . . servant?"

CHARLES KINGSLEY

Our sages recommended
that a father should spend
less than his means on food,
up to his means on dress,
and beyond his means for
his wife and children.

MAIMONIDES

A man cannot leave a better legacy
to the world than a
well-educated family.

THOMAS SCOTT

A family is the first and essential cell
of human society.

POPE JOHN XXIII

Keep your family from the
abominable practice
of backbiting.

THE OLD FARMER'S ALMANAC, 1811

Family

Through the survival of their
    children, happy parents are able
    to think calmly, and with a very
practical affection, of a world in which
    they are to have no direct share.

WALTER PATER

The family you come from isn't
    as important as the family
    you're going to have.

RING LARDNER

A family is a unit composed
not only of children, but of men,
    women, an occasional animal,
    and the common cold.

OGDEN NASH

Courage

Young children, when they are afraid, turn to their fathers for comfort. When fathers respond with strength and assurance, they demonstrate to their children the importance of courage.

Sir Winston Churchill writes, "Courage is the first of human qualities because it is the quality which guarantees all the others." In this chapter, we consider this "first human quality" and the way it touches every aspect of our lives.

All happiness depends on
courage and work.

HONORÉ DE BALZAC

Courage is a kind of salvation.

PLATO

Despair is an evil counselor.

SIR WALTER SCOTT

Courage and perseverance
have a magical talisman, before
which difficulties disappear and
obstacles vanish into thin air.

JOHN QUINCY ADAMS

Facing it — always facing it —
that's the way to get through.

JOSEPH CONRAD

The first and great
commandment
is don't let them
scare you.

ELMER DAVIS

Without courage, wisdom
bears no fruit.

BALTASAR GRACIÁN

God grant me the courage
not to give up what I think is right,
even if I think it is hopeless.

CHESTER NIMITZ

Courage conquers all things.

OVID

Courage is its own reward.

PLAUTUS

Fortune favors the brave.

TERENCE

Fear corrupts.

JOHN STEINBECK

Fear is an illusion.

MICHAEL JORDAN

Courage is doing what you're
afraid to do. There can be no
courage unless you're scared.

EDWARD RICKENBACKER

We cannot solve problems except
by solving them.

M. SCOTT PECK

When you get to the end of
your rope, tie a knot and hang on.

FRANKLIN D. ROOSEVELT

Courage is being scared to death — and saddling up anyway.

JOHN WAYNE

Courage is always the surest wisdom.

WINSTON CHURCHILL

FATHER'S LESSON #4

Hope

A wise father takes care to nurture his child's hopes and dreams. It is a fortunate son or daughter who learns the power of optimism through the words and deeds of a positive, supportive family.

Dreamers change the world, optimists make the best partners, and hope is the mainspring of life. On the pages that follow, we consider fatherly advice about the power of big dreams.

What you can
do or dream
you can do,
begin it.
Boldness has
genius, power,
and magic in it.

GOETHE

In adversity, a man is saved by hope.

MENANDER

Live from miracle to miracle.

ARTUR RUBINSTEIN

Faith is the antiseptic of the soul.

WALT WHITMAN

Honor
begets honor;
trust begets trust;
faith begets faith,
and hope is the
mainspring of life.

HENRY LEWIS STIMSON

To persevere, trusting in what
hopes he has, is courage in a man.

EURIPIDES

Faith begins where reason
sinks exhausted.

ALBERT PIKE

In actual life every great enterprise
begins with and takes its
first forward step in faith.

FRIEDRICH VON SCHLEGEL

Perpetual optimism is
a force multiplier.

COLIN POWELL

If you think you can win,
you can win. Faith is necessary
to victory.

WILLIAM HAZLITT

Faith is not believing that
God can, but that God will!

ABRAHAM LINCOLN

Alas! The fearful unbelief is unbelief in yourself.

THOMAS CARLYLE

Begin to weave, and God will
provide the thread.
GERMAN PROVERB

Nothing is impossible to
a willing heart.
JOHN HEYWOOD

Never take away hope
from any man.
OLIVER WENDELL HOLMES, SR.

Great hopes make great men.

THOMAS FULLER

Worry
and anxiety
are sand in the
machinery of life;
faith is the oil.

E. STANLEY JONES

FATHER'S LESSON #5

Work

Wise fathers understand the high correlation between hard work and rich rewards. That's why diligent dads demonstrate and declare the value of a good day's work.

General Colin Powell advises, "There are no secrets to success: Don't waste time looking for them. Success is the result of perfection, hard work, learning from failure, loyalty to those for whom you work, and persistence." Thoughtful fathers agree, and hopefully their children will, too.

Work for your soul's sake.

EDGAR LEE MASTERS

Each man's talent is his call.
There is one direction in which
all doors are open to him.

RALPH WALDO EMERSON

Think enthusiastically about
everything, especially your work.

NORMAN VINCENT PEALE

Work joyfully and peacefully,
knowing that right thoughts and
right efforts will inevitably bring
about right results.

JAMES ALLEN

When troubles arise, wise men go to their work.

ELBERT HUBBARD

Diligence makes good luck.

BEN FRANKLIN

Begin — to begin is half the work.

AUSONIUS

Be like a postage stamp:
   Stick to one thing till
      you get there.

JOSH BILLINGS

It is easier to do a job right than to explain why you didn't.

MARTIN VAN BUREN

The more I want to get something
done, the less I call it work.

RICHARD BACH

Nothing is really work unless
you would rather be doing
something else.

JAMES MATTHEW BARRIE

Do your work with your whole
heart, and you will succeed —
there is so little competition.

ELBERT HUBBARD

I've always believed that if
you put in the work,
the results will come.

MICHAEL JORDAN

If my life had been made up of
eight-hour days, I do not believe I
could have accomplished
a great deal.

THOMAS EDISON

Like what you do. If you don't
like it, do something else.

PAUL HARVEY

Honesty

Honesty is woven into the fabric of human relationships, and it can never be removed without tearing that fabric apart. Therefore, thoughtful fathers teach the value of honesty just as surely as they teach their children to read and write.

In this chapter, we consider the honor of behaving honorably. For a fatherly lesson in fidelity, please turn the page.

Never mind your happiness.
Do your duty.

WILL DURANT

A quiet conscience
makes one so serene.

BYRON

If a man seeks greatness,
let him forget greatness and
ask for truth, and he
will find both.

HORACE MANN

Fame is vapor, popularity an accident, riches take wings. Only one thing endures and that is character.

HORACE GREELEY

Truth will rise above falsehood
as oil above water.

CERVANTES

Of all the properties which
belong to honorable men, not one
is so highly prized as
that of character.

HENRY CLAY

Reason often makes mistakes,
but conscience never does.

JOSH BILLINGS

Today, I am going to give you two
tests: one on trigonometry and
one on honesty. I hope you
pass them both, but if
you must fail one, let it
be trigonometry.

MADISON SARRATT

Character, not circumstances,
makes the man.

BOOKER T. WASHINGTON

Simplicity of character is the
natural result of profound thought.

WILLIAM HAZLITT

Dare to be honest
and fear no labor.
ROBERT BURNS

A man of character finds a special
attractiveness in difficulty,
since it is only by coming to grips
with difficulty that he can
realize his potentialities.
CHARLES DeGAULLE

First honesty, then industry.
ANDREW CARNEGIE

Wherever a man goes to dwell,
his character goes with him.

AFRICAN PROVERB

Two things profoundly impress me:
the starry heavens above me and
the moral law within me.

IMMANUEL KANT

Honest hearts produce
honest actions.

BRIGHAM YOUNG

We do not need more knowledge,
   we need more character!

CALVIN COOLIDGE

The most dangerous of all
   falsehoods is a slightly
   distorted truth.

G. C. LICHTENBERG

Have patience awhile;
   slanders are not long-lived.
   Truth is the child of time;
   before long she shall
   appear to vindicate you.

IMMANUEL KANT

If you shut up truth, and bury it
underground, it will but grow.

EMILE ZOLA

Truth will be uppermost one time
or another, like cork, though kept
down in the water.

WILLIAM TEMPLE

If you tell the truth, you don't
have to remember anything.

MARK TWAIN

Tell the truth,
and so puzzle
and confound
your adversaries.

HENRY WOTTON

Persistence

Life is a marathon, not a sprint. And every day, we are given countless opportunities to quit. But wise fathers understand — and teach — the power of persistence.

Jean Jacques Rousseau observes, "To endure is the first thing that a child ought to learn, and that which he will have the most need to know." The quotations in this chapter provide additional energy to serious marathoners who find themselves happily engaged in the endurance race called life.

Every noble work is at first impossible.

THOMAS CARLYLE

Never, never, never give in.

WINSTON CHURCHILL

It does not matter how slowly
  you go so long as you do not stop.

CONFUCIUS

The block of granite, which is
an obstacle in the pathway of
the weak, becomes a stepping-stone
  in the pathway of the strong.

THOMAS CARLYLE

Victory belongs to
  the most persevering.

NAPOLEON I

He who labors diligently
need never despair; for all
things are accomplished
by diligence and labor.

MENANDER

I am not the smartest or the most
talented person in the world, but I
succeeded because I kept going, and
going, and going.

SYLVESTER STALLONE

You do what you can for as long
as you can, and when you finally
can't, you do the next best thing.
You back up, but you don't give up.

CHUCK YEAGER

Nothing in the world can take
the place of persistence. Talent
will not. . . . Genius will not . . . .
Education will not . . . .
Persistence and determination
alone are omnipotent.

CALVIN COOLIDGE

Diligence overcomes difficulties;
sloth makes them.

BEN FRANKLIN

There is no royal road to anything.
Do one thing at a time and all
things in succession. That
which grows slowly, endures.

JOSIAH G. HOLLAND

He conquers who endures.

PERSIUS

We will either find a way or make one.

Hannibal

Happiness

All loving fathers have the same wish for their children: happiness. But discerning dads know that happiness is paradoxical: The faster we race after it, the more elusive it seems.

Once we stop racing breathlessly after happiness — and concentrate on meeting the demands of life and the needs of others — happiness finds us, as the following quotations will attest.

The happiness
of your life
depends on
the quality of
your thoughts.

MARCUS AURELIUS ANTONINUS

We create our own happiness.

HENRY DAVID THOREAU

What we call the secret
of happiness is no more
a secret than our willingness
to choose life.

LEO BUSCAGLIA

When we recall the past, we
usually find that it is the simplest
things — not the great occasions —
that in retrospect give off the
greatest glow of happiness.

BOB HOPE

Happiness grows at our own
firesides and is not to be picked
in strangers' gardens.

DOUGLAS JERROLD

Happiness is a habit. Cultivate it.

ELBERT HUBBARD

Derive happiness in oneself from a
good day's work, from illuminating
the fog that surrounds us.

HENRI MATISSE

When work is a pleasure, life is
a joy! When work is a duty,
life is slavery.

MAXIM GORKY

Happiness lies in the joy of
achievement and the thrill
of creative effort.

FRANKLIN D. ROOSEVELT

Joy is
not in things,
it is in us.

RICHARD WAGNER

Most people are about as happy
as they make up their minds to be.
ABRAHAM LINCOLN

The foolish man seeks happiness
in the distance, the wise grows it
under his feet.
J. ROBERT OPPENHEIMER

True happiness is not attained
through self-gratification
but through fidelity
to a worthy cause.
THOMAS JEFFERSON

A sad soul can kill you far quicker than a germ.

JOHN STEINBECK

Everyone
chases after
happiness, not
noticing that
happiness is
at their heels.

BERTOLT BRECHT

Don't mistake pleasure for happiness.

JOSH BILLINGS

The happiest people are those who do the most for others.

BOOKER T. WASHINGTON

Life

First, fathers give their children the gift of life; then, they show their children how to live it. As they touch the lives of their sons and daughters in countless ways, fathers change the world one child at a time.

In this concluding chapter, we share lifetime lessons of fatherly proportions. As you read these words and consider your own behavior, remember that your father is *still* changing the world — through you.

The tragedy
of life is not
so much what
men suffer as
what they miss.

THOMAS CARLYLE

We find in life exactly what
we put in it.
RALPH WALDO EMERSON

Make your life a mission —
not an intermission.
ARNOLD GLASOW

Plunge boldly into the thick of life!
GOETHE

Life is a journey, not a destination.
Happiness is not "there," but here,
not tomorrow, but today.

SIDNEY GREENBERG

Do not take life too seriously.
You'll never get out of it alive.

ELBERT HUBBARD

Assume responsibility for the quality of your own life.

NORMAN COUSINS

This time, like all times, is a very
good one if we only know
what to do with it.

RALPH WALDO EMERSON

The art of living is like all arts;
it must be learned and practiced
with incessant care.

GOETHE

Begin at once to live,
and count each day a separate life.

SENECA

No matter how long you live,
die young.

ELBERT HUBBARD

A man is never old until regrets
take the place of his dreams.

JOHN BARRYMORE

The greatest use of a life is to spend
it for something that
will outlast it.

WILLIAM JAMES

Life consists not in holding
good cards, but in playing well
those you do hold.

JOSH BILLINGS

The chief danger in life is that you
may take too many precautions.

ALFRED ADLER

If you're not in the parade,
you watch the parade.
That's life.

MIKE DITKA

Life is
a lively process
of becoming.

Douglas MacArthur

Life is an error-making and an
error-correcting process.

JONAS SALK

Life is a succession of lessons
enforced by immediate reward,
or, oftener, by immediate
chastisement.

ERNEST DIMNET

I take a simple view of life:
keep your eyes open and
get on with it.

LAURENCE OLIVIER

What would life be if we had no
courage to attempt anything?

VINCENT VAN GOGH

Every man's life is a fairy tale
written by God's fingers.

HANS CHRISTIAN ANDERSEN

To be able to look back upon one's
past life with satisfaction
is to live twice.

JOHN DALBERG ACTON

Time is
a circus always
packing up and
moving away.

BEN HECHT

The longer
I live, the
more beautiful
life becomes.

FRANK LLOYD WRIGHT

Find the journey's end in every step.

RALPH WALDO EMERSON

Sources

Sources

Sources

Sources

About the Author

Criswell Freeman is a Doctor of Clinical Psychology who lives, writes and works in Nashville, Tennessee. Dr. Freeman is also the author of *The Wisdom Series* published by Walnut Grove Press. *The Wisdom Series* is a collection of inspirational quotation books. In addition to his work as a writer, Freeman also hosts the nationally syndicated radio program *Wisdom Made in America.*

About
DELANEY STREET PRESS

DELANEY STREET PRESS publishes a series of books designed to inspire and entertain readers of all ages. DELANEY STREET books are distributed by Walnut Grove Press. For more information, call 800-256-8584.